The Essential Guide for Teachers in International Schools

by
Mary Langford, Richard Pearce,
Debra Rader, Coreen Sears

Illustrations by
Richard Caston

Published 2002 by John Catt Educational Ltd
Great Glemham, Saxmundham, Suffolk IP17 2DH
Tel: +44 (0) 1728 663666   Fax: +44 (0) 1728 663415
E-mail: enquiries@johncatt.co.uk   Internet: http://www.johncatt.com

© 2002 John Catt Educational Ltd

All rights reserved. No part of this publication may be reproduced, stored in a retrieval system, transmitted in any form or by any means, electronic, mechanical, photocopying, recording, or otherwise, without the prior permission of the publishers.

Opinions expressed in this publication are those of the contributors, and are not necessarily those of the publishers or the sponsors. We cannot accept responsibility for any errors or omissions.

The Sex Discrimination Act 1975. The publishers have taken all reasonable steps to avoid a contravention of Section 38 of the Sex Discrimination Act 1975. However, it should be noted that (save where there is an express provision to the contrary) where words have been used which denote the masculine gender only, they shall, pursuant and subject to the said Act, for the purpose of this publication, be deemed to include the feminine gender and *vice versa*.

A CIP catalogue record for this book is available from the British Library.

ISBN: 0 901577 79 0

Designed and typeset by John Catt Educational Limited,
Great Glemham, Saxmundham, Suffolk IP17 2DH

Printed and bound in Great Britain by Bell & Bain Ltd, 303 Burnfield Road, Thornliebank, Glasgow G46 7UQ, Scotland.

Contents

Foreword	4
Introduction	6
1 Living abroad	7
2 The nature of international schools	11
How international schools work	11
Colleagues and the staff room	16
Life in the classroom	22
3 The nature of international school families	35
Expatriate families	35
International school parents	38
International school children	42
Host country families	48
4 Programme and curriculum	49
Introduction	49
Pedagogy	49
Materials	51
Assessment	52
Primary School	53
Middle and High School (Secondary)	54
Schools with bilingual programmes	57
Need for differentiated instruction	57
Special Educational Needs	58
Beyond the classroom	62
Professional development opportunities	62
Postscript: humour/humor	63
References	64

Foreword

A companion on your journey...

You have chosen the adventurer's path: teaching in an international school.

This had also been, in most cases many years ago, the choice of all the participants at the very first European Council of International Schools (ECIS) Cross-Cultural Conference entitled *Teaching – Understanding Other Cultures* (Düsseldorf, March 2001). The presentations, exercises and exchanges on intercultural awareness and skills were eye-openers. Gradually many of the tricky situations encountered in host countries or at new schools as well as feelings and reactions became so much more understandable.

One of the outcomes of the conference was the common desire to offer a roadmap to other or future international schoolteachers as part of an induction programme. A very strong cross-cultural component would best invite the teacher to observe, to reflect and to learn.

Four well-known and experienced authors in the field, Mary Langford, Richard Pearce, Debra Rader and Coreen Sears, offered to work together on a guide, which is the most important part of the programme. You will immediately notice that they deliberately wrote in a highly readable style, for native and non-native English readers.

It was the illustrator Richard Caston who ended up with the biggest problem: how to draw people without stereotyping in one way or another? Finally he decided it would be slightly less controversial to draw animals instead of humans. Any resemblance to existing people is purely coincidental, of course!

After having read this book, you will surely join me in being very grateful to the four authors and the illustrator who voluntarily shared their expertise. From its inception, this ambitious project was supported by ECIS. This book in your hands has been printed for ECIS and is a sign of the paramount importance intercultural awareness and skills have for the largest association of international schools in the world.

Foreword

The journey is yours and yours alone, as is the journey of each of the international students you are or will be teaching and coaching. May this book not only be a roadmap but also a lantern on your road to understanding and interacting with other cultures in an international environment.

Beatrice Larose
Chairperson of the ECIS Cross-Cultural Committee 1998-2001

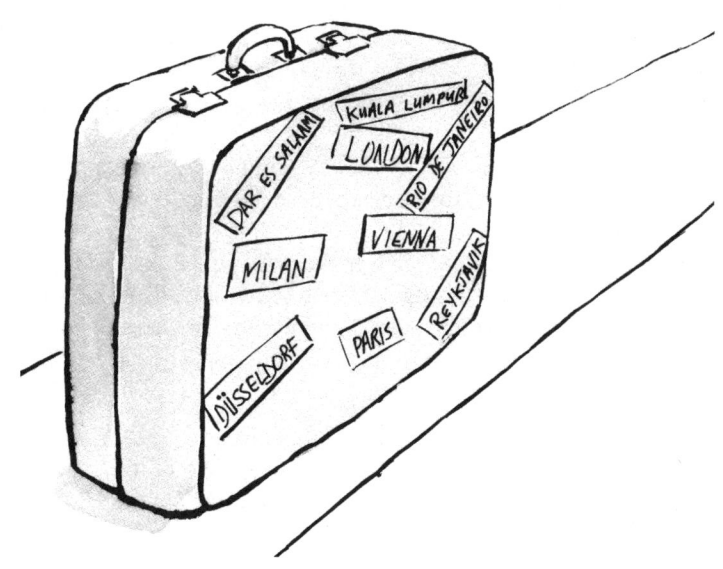

Introduction

"...travel is fatal to prejudice, bigotry and narrow-mindedness... broad, wholesome, charitable views of men and things cannot be acquired by vegetating in one corner of the earth all one's lifetime."

Mark Twain

We all know that first impressions are lasting impressions: you meet your new colleagues, the children, the parents, the whole school community before you have had time to get the hang of things, but everyone gets formative impressions from those first meetings. So here are some points that we think need to be known first. Some of them may not apply to your school, but they may still apply to the school your students have just left, which still frames the picture in their – and their parents' – minds. We suggest you read them before term begins and look back at them again as experience puts flesh on the bones of your expectations.

You are competent and experienced at home, and keen to apply your teaching skills, but you can hardly believe how many things can be different in the school you are joining. We are not trying to tell you all the differences – just to suggest where differences may be hiding. If they take you by surprise, especially if several appear at once, it can cast a shadow over your whole outlook and make you see the downside of everything. What will carry you through is your professionalism, your determination to do the best for your students, and your readiness to think about other ways of doing things which may be more appropriate than the ways you are used to.

If you are an old hand, you know about this already. You moved abroad, you had new experiences, you had some shocks. Would this have helped you in the few weeks before or immediately after arriving in that first school? That is the aim of this book. As everyone said when you first went abroad, please tell us how you get on!

Chapter 1

Living abroad

"What kind of a bird are you if you can't sing?" chirped the bird.
"What kind of a bird are you if you can't swim?", retorted the duck.

Peter and the Wolf, Sergei Prokofiev

Working abroad presents an exciting opportunity for any teacher. It brings new meaning to 'lifelong learning'.

There will be many good things about the experience:

- a new professional challenge – perhaps for the first time in an overseas school that will be very different to the national schools you may previously have experienced;
- new friends and colleagues who will generally be quite interesting people in themselves (after all, seeking a job abroad suggests a certain sense of adventure);
- an opportunity to live in a new country, often with a different culture and language to be learned, and perhaps the possibility of travel.

Equally there will be challenges and frustrations:

- a new school means learning new systems and procedures;
- colleagues of differing nationalities and pedagogical backgrounds may have unusual perspectives and attitudes that you have not previously encountered;
- living in a foreign country and cultural environment, particularly with a different language, means that even the most simple and basic life skills may have to be relearned.

A common response to the adaptation process associated with an overseas move is culture shock. The experts say that initially expatriates are likely to experience a euphoric honeymoon phase: everything is exciting and interesting and exotic. When this wears off, it can become downright annoying, and this (two to four months after arrival) is when you may enter the slippery slope of homesickness and even depression.

Then, as you come to adjust to the new place and begin to settle by making friends and learning how to manage the basics, you start to enjoy life. (Despite this 'model' for adaptation, you may find that you experience the occasional high or low when you least expect it.) There are various publications that address the 'expatriate experience' and it may be helpful to read some of these so that you can anticipate your reactions to the move.

Some people never experience anything as drastic as culture shock. There are some preventative strategies:

1. Learn a few basic phrases in the new language. Learn how to *say* them and how to *read* them – this will be important for your 'survival'. Even though English is becoming a dominant language throughout the world, it is still courteous to make an effort to communicate in the host country language. Once you have mastered the basics, and if you feel motivated to do so, consider taking classes in the language. It may be that your school can help you with this: some international schools offer classes to new teachers, or perhaps the parent association provides this for new parents and you can join in.

2. Find ways to become involved with the local people and culture. In all too many overseas schools, teachers become reliant on their colleagues for their social life, and it can be limiting. If you have a hobby you can pursue in the local community, go for it! For example, you could try evening art or cooking classes, local sports teams, folk dancing, bridge groups, choirs

or orchestras, *etc*. Don't exclude the 'expatriate' bodies such as the churches or cultural societies as these may provide you with some fellow expatriate contacts beyond the school gate. The more you engage in the local community, the more quickly you will begin to settle. Ask your new colleagues at school about such opportunities.

3. Acquaint yourself with the 'self-help' publications available to expatriates living in the country. There are now guides written for most countries in the world. There may be city guides – not just the touristy ones, but guides written for expatriate residents (though the touristy ones are important so that you get to know the country!). Sometimes these publications are not widely available, but may be distributed by organisations such as local churches, or even the PTA. Ask your new school for recommendations, and start reading *before* you move! Then re-read the guides after you arrive and they become more relevant.

4. It may be wise to ascertain whether women are treated as equal to men, and if not, how that would affect your life there.

5. Make the most of the orientation documents and services provided by the school. What is on offer will vary greatly between schools, but anything you can read will be helpful to you. Your school may assign you an official mentor, another experienced teacher, to help you learn the ropes. If this is not the practice, you may nonetheless identify a colleague who may become an 'unofficial' mentor to help you. Take advantage of any induction programmes at school. You may find at the time that these matters seem a bit tedious. Later you may find that the information they provide helps to accelerate your adjustment process.

6. Be sure to register with a doctor, dentist and any other health care specialists you may require as soon as you arrive (your school will probably have a list). Don't leave this until you are having a problem! Also, if it is recommended, be sure you register with your embassy or consulate.

7. Ask questions. Keep a list of questions and research the answers in the materials provided by the school. If you cannot find the answers yourself, ask the school.

It is a good idea to learn who does what at your new school. You will probably find that the head's secretary and the business office manager are key players in helping you find the answers to these questions.

Essentail check list:

- How are your working papers managed (work permits are required in many places) and how do you register with local authorities (if necessary)?
- Shipping personal goods (and finding out in advance how much of your own educational resources you should bring along).
- Finding accommodation (including the first few days you are there).
- Health, contents and home insurance.
- Registering with a doctor and dentist (and any other specialists that you may require – *eg* optometrist, gynaecologist).
- Driving licences and getting a car or, alternatively, public transport options.
- Opening a bank account.
- Tax situation.
- Benefits offered by the school.
- What is the cost of living?
- What is the school's position *vis-à-vis* your partner and/or your children? Is your partner eligible for employment?
- Cash lifeline with your home country/bank (how to get money in a hurry).

Remember, flexibility, adaptability and patience are virtues. So if you regard yourself as a lifelong learner, you've come to the right place!

Chapter 2

The nature of international schools

"There's nobody normal in this class."

IB Year 1 student

How international schools work

International schools are a unique genre of educational institution. While no two international schools are the same, there are some common characteristics that distinguish them from national schools. Some of them may be linked through regional organisations such as the European

Now why is 'my' food nowhere to be found?

Council of International Schools (ECIS). While most so-called international schools are English-medium, 'western style' schools, there are exceptions. Many articles and research papers have been written in an effort to define international schools, but we will summarise the characteristics in this section. Your school will probably fit into one or more of these categories.

The nature of international schools

Not only are the buildings quite different...

What's different from one school to the next?

Historic origin, educational philosophy and language

Management structure and decision-makers

Admissions procedures and criteria

Terminology and nomenclature

Timetables, schedules, calendars and holidays

Buildings and physical environment

Curriculum, teaching methodology, assessment

Size, population and cultural diversity of the student body

Relationship with the host country

Historical origins of international schools

1. Schools founded to serve the needs of expatriate communities, such as:
   - a multi-national expatriate community (*eg* diplomats in a capital city or financial services professionals in a financial centre); or
   - an expatriate community dominated by one nationality (*eg* a national industry-based professional community such as petroleum industry, or an agricultural business dominated by only a few nationalities).

2. Schools founded by foreign missionaries seeking to introduce (for example) Christian faith and values to a local community.
3. Schools established by local nationals who believed that by offering their children a 'foreign' education (*eg* French, British, American or IB) they may have better access to foreign universities.

The various management structures of (and differing jargon used in) international schools

Many international schools are privately owned by one or more individuals. Some are co-operatives. Others are established as foundations, charities or non-profit institutions – perhaps with historic ties to a sponsoring embassy or embassies – and are overseen by governors, trustees or boards appointed in different ways to serve varying terms of office. The day-to-day management responsibilities may be vested in a superintendent, director, head, principal, or head teacher. Responsibilities may be divided in a variety of ways, with employees with differing job titles. Suffice it to say that institutional jargon can vary significantly from one school to the next and it is important that you figure out which terms are used in your school! Confusion over such matters could lead to embarrassment: imagine thinking that as a teacher of Year 1 you would be working with six-year-olds (or five-year-olds), only to discover that you are working with eleven-year-olds!

Examples of international school jargon

Nursery school, early childhood, early years, pre-school, primary school, elementary school, junior school, lower school, middle school, junior high school, secondary school, upper school, lower house, upper house, middle years, sixth form college, high school, grade, form, class, year group, teacher, faculty, staff, tutor, homeroom teacher, advisor.

Differences in facilities, size and nationality

Facilities are also varied. While some schools offer purpose-built, state-of-the-art campuses others have been adapted to school use – more extreme examples include former castles or palaces, factories, hotels, prisons, campsites and office buildings. These properties may have been adapted as effectively and imaginatively as possible, but may nonetheless cause some restrictions that creative and flexible staff members have to overcome! If your classroom were to have an en-suite bathroom, just what would *you* do with the tub? Still, teaching in a former prison or palace can lead to interesting experiences and you might be able to dine out on the stories when you next visit your friends and family back home!

School sizes and populations also differ. A school may be located on two or three sites, not necessarily very close to one another. Some schools may have fewer than 100 pupils, others approaching 2000. In a smaller school, you may find that you are the only teacher of a particular subject, or of a particular grade or year group, or that you are teaching a mixed-age group. Some schools are dominated by a single nationality; others are highly diverse with no predominant nationality whilst host-country nationals may heavily populate other schools. The nationality make-up of the teaching staff may be similarly diverse. Schools may be characterised by highly transient expatriate children and faculty where the average stay is two to three years. The degree and frequency of turnover in student population may help to determine the teaching methodology used, particularly the extent to which teachers are expected to differentiate the curriculum to accommodate newly-arrived pupils.

Faculty input in the management of international schools

The role of teachers and faculty in the management and decision-making process differs greatly between schools. In some schools, because of local tradition or employment law, teachers may be elected to serve on councils that help to determine employment practice. In other schools, teachers may have a more informal and consultative role in management decisions. In other situations, management may be quite hierarchical with the head making most of the decisions without teacher involvement.

The role of parents

The role of parents also varies between schools, but it is fair to say that in general, international schools are inclusive of parents and have active parent associations involved in many facets of school life.

The variety of curricula, programmes, school timetables and calendars

The curriculum varies between schools and sometimes even within schools – it may be American, British, French, International Baccalaureate (IB), or host country – or a combination of the above. The provision of specialist programmes and learning support varies tremendously – some schools have armies of specialists supporting the programme, whereas in other schools a classroom teacher may also teach PE, art and music – and cook lunch! Admissions procedures and criteria differ – sometimes based on the applicant's passport, ability, or even the parent's professional affiliation.

The organisation of the timetable/schedule and school year may be dictated by the host country or historical traditions of the school. Host country holidays may be observed while your own national holidays may not. Start times, length of day and length of school year may vary – some schools have three terms, others two semesters.

Induction into the school and integration into the community

International schools have different techniques for inducting new staff as well as new pupils. You may be fortunate to work in a school where there is a well-developed induction and orientation programme for staff with ample support and mentoring in place to help you avoid most of the pitfalls. Others may not offer as much, and you may find yourself struggling with basic situations. Be sure to avail yourself of all the information and support offered at your school.

Depending on the host country, your school may be well integrated into the local culture, economy and environment or, conversely, it may seem like an expatriate island in a foreign setting; it may even be located in a segregated compound. This may be in part due to local law, tradition or religion. In some countries, host nationals are forbidden from attending international schools. In others, the local government may actively discourage the international school community from interacting with locals. Cultural differences may make integration virtually impossible. Security and protection of foreign nationals could be an issue. Teachers should become aware of what their school's particular circumstances are, for the sake of their pupils' as well as their own personal safety.

In conclusion, each international school has its own history, purpose, procedures, style and culture. Open-mindedness, observation, and flexibility are the key to understanding your own school.

Colleagues and the staff room

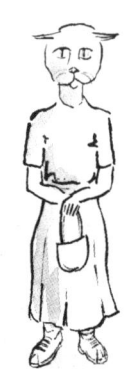

...feeling so different...

Many international schools employ teachers who are experienced in delivering the type of programme that the school offers. Others are forced by local circumstances to employ teachers who are unaccustomed to the programme of the school. Even where there is a degree of shared experience, however, you may be struck by the many differences among your colleagues in the ways they lead their professional lives.

Training and experience

Non-national teachers who work in international schools fall into four main categories:

1. Teachers (often young, but not always) who plan to spend two or three years abroad, perhaps in a series of international schools, as a way of seeing the world and widening their professional experience.

2. Teachers who are not nationals of the host country but who live there permanently – perhaps they are married to a host country national. This group tends to make up the longer-term members of a school's staff.

3. Teachers who are accompanying partners/spouses who have taken up an expatriate posting.

4. Teachers who teach the host country language and other foreign languages who are employed specifically because of the languages they speak.

Teachers from this variety of backgrounds and cultures, not surprisingly, arrive in a school bringing differences of experience and training. Many international schools, in truth, harbour at least one teacher with views about education that border on the eccentric. However, we are not talking here about major issues relating to differences of programme and curriculum. These are dealt with elsewhere in this book. What we are concerned with in this section is the variation in the ways that teachers deliver similar material, and differences of style and custom.

Differences in teaching methods

You may notice the following variations in this area:

- The level of dependence on textbooks;
- How much use is made of publisher's materials such as worksheets;
- How much use is made of teacher-created materials;
- The amount of whole class teaching;
- The use of instructional groupings;
- How teachers allot grades or marks – you will notice, for instance, that teachers from some backgrounds award more As than others;
- The amount of homework given;
- To what extent teachers acknowledge the cultural and linguistic diversity in a classroom;
- The degree of access to the Internet – in some systems it is customary to screen the material that students can access;
- How much independence teachers give to the student learners;
- How much choice is given to students in the ways they learn.

You may find that teachers of foreign languages use a different methodology from that found in schools in English-speaking countries. This difference frequently reflects a more traditional, grammar-based approach to language teaching. For teacher colleagues, the impact of these differences is only significant in schools with bilingual programmes.

Differences of terminology

You will notice immediately many variations in how teachers from different backgrounds refer to aspects of school life. Some of the differences are quite slight: they are simply using different names for mutually understood concepts. The following short list gives some examples of terminology:

- Recess/break/playtime;
- Refectory/dining-room/cafeteria/lunchroom;
- Timetable/schedule;
- Faculty/teaching staff;
- Auditions/try-outs;
- Special needs/SEN/Resource/Learning Support;
- ESL/ESOL/EAL/EFL/Extra English.

Other variations of terminology may mask more significant differences: the variety of ways of naming year levels in a school, for instance. What age of child is taught in which class is important for you to know since parents too are confused by the naming system and often want to know why their child has been placed in an apparently higher or lower class.

Teachers generally become used to these changes of terminology quite quickly. One or two teachers in every school, though, stick fiercely to what they know. This is another area where it is wise to be flexible and open-minded!

Differences of style and approach

You may notice some of the following areas where style and approach are different:

- What teachers view as acceptable behaviour;
- How teachers achieve discipline;
- Approaches to class 'problems';
- What is acceptable dress;
- The relationship between teachers and children and teachers and parents;
- What is an acceptable way to address an adult or a child;
- What is considered to be 'polite' behaviour.

You may find that you need to adjust your behaviour to bring it in line with the expectations of the school. It is also very worthwhile observing how effective and experienced teachers in your new school handle their interaction with students, parents and colleagues.

Maintaining confidence in yourself

Sometimes, in the face of all these differences, it is easy for new teachers to feel unsure about their own ability to cope and to adapt. You need to remember, though, that all teachers in international schools have had to move through the same learning process. Most emerge at the other side of the process of adaptation feeling comfortable in their new environment and having added a range of new skills and understandings to their professional repertoire. Once again, you should not hesitate to ask successful 'old hands' about any facet of school life that is unfamiliar to you.

Life in the staff room/faculty lounge/teachers' room

The staff room in every school has its unique atmosphere. In general, staff rooms in international schools tend to be social and friendly places where teachers can relax and talk about general school concerns. Also, you will find that, frequently, there are delicious snacks on offer. Indeed, every function at an international school tends to be accompanied by eating and drinking. Perhaps this is why losing weight and visiting the gym are such common topics of conversation in our staff rooms!

One or two features that may be new to you are typical of international school staff rooms. In some school systems it would be unthinkable that a parent would come into the staff room. In international schools the line between teachers and parents is not as clear cut and it is not unusual for a parent to come into the staff room to look for a teacher or to use the staff photocopier. Sometimes, too, small groups of parents in school for a meeting come into the staff room to pick up a cup of coffee. Once again, you are wise to accept the custom that obtains in your school, rather than to work against it.

Something else you may notice is a tendency for certain groups of teachers to avoid mixing in a general way with the rest of the staff. This, unfortunately, may arise from a difference in their terms of employment. Locally hired teachers in some schools, often teachers of the host country language or physical education, may feel themselves to be somewhat outside the mainstream of school life. It is always possible, and very worthwhile, to cross this barrier and to take the trouble to build up a collegial relationship with all your colleagues.

The nature of international schools

"Sometimes it seems so impossible to communicate with them..."

Making friends among new and established teachers is one way of receiving and offering support in your new surroundings. Frequently, new teachers make trips together to buy furniture for their new homes or to investigate the possibilities of the new location.

Many teachers in home systems prefer to find their social life outside school. In an expatriate location, however, spending social time with colleagues is an effective means of getting over the initial adjustment period. Some of these colleagues may become long-term friends with whom you choose to spend much of your free time. In any case, creating a social framework in the early days will provide you with a springboard for pursuing your hobbies and interests and for extending your social circle.

Differences in staff room behaviour

There are some significant differences in the way teachers from different backgrounds and cultures behave in their common meeting places, and it is useful to observe what is the custom in your particular school.

Teachers from some countries are very hesitant about discussing individual students in the staff room. From their point of view, this is disrespectful to the student and appears rather unprofessional. Teachers from other backgrounds use the staff room to let off steam about a particular student, often using quite strong language. What might not be apparent is the degree of professional and personal commitment that such a teacher brings to his/her work with students – they are simply sharing temporary frustrations in order to return to the classroom refreshed and re-focused.

Neither behaviour is 'right' or 'better'; it is solely a difference of custom. It is difficult, though, in cases where a colleague's behaviour might really offend. Successful teachers in international schools somehow manage to remain true to their own training and beliefs without looking or acting as if they dislike the behaviour of others. Probably both groups will need to temper their behaviour depending on the culture of the individual school. We need principled flexibility and tolerance to work happily in our many-cultured settings.

Parents as colleagues

Something that may be different for some new teachers is the presence in the staff room of a fair number of colleagues who are also parents of children in the school.

The presence of these teaching parents has a certain impact on life in the staff room and your relationship with them as colleagues. Fortunately, most of these parents learn to separate the two halves of their lives quite successfully, and save concerns about their children for private conversation with the teacher in question. You may find a need, however, to pre-empt any tendency for teacher parents to talk about their children's academic work in the staff room, by making a point of fixing appointments elsewhere for these discussions.

We depend on teaching parents to be discreet and positive about all aspects of the school and their child's education when talking to people who are not staff members. International schools tend to lie at the heart of small communities where gossip and negative remarks can cause great damage.

Non-teaching colleagues

In most international schools, the administrative personnel and school maintenance staff are normally recruited from the local community. The presence of host country nationals offers a cultural richness and linguistic variety to life in school as well as supplying an element of longer-term stability. One of the pleasant aspects of many international schools is that such staff tend to be very much part of the team and are included in all school events and social occasions. These colleagues can also supply you with practical information and insights into local modes of living that will be invaluable.

Life in the classroom

Introduction: The make-up of the class

Classes in international schools contain students who are different from each other in very many ways. This is because each student has a unique family, cultural, linguistic and educational history due to the move or moves they and their families have made.

Naturally with this diversity among your students, they and their families will have varying views and experiences relating to education. Different cultures view education in different ways and their education systems reflect those views. In an international school class, it is common to find students who have differing expectations and experiences relating to the following features of school life:

- The age at which formal education begins;
- The age at which students start to learn to read and write;
- How students are taught to read;
- The number of students in a class;
- The arrangement of desks;
- The relationship between teacher and students;
- What is considered good behaviour in the classroom;
- How discipline is maintained;
- The overall approach to teaching and learning;
- The use of textbooks;
- How students are assessed (examination or portfolio assessment, for instance);
- The amount of homework assigned;
- The place of problem-solving and critical thinking;
- The use of independent research projects;
- The use of information technology;
- The kinds and number of after-school and social activities arranged for students.

The following grid sets out some typical attitudes and experiences of students and parents from two of the cultures from which our students come. It may be illuminating to list student differences in your own class in a similar way.

The nature of international schools

Education system	Korean	Finnish			
Age at which formal education begins	5 years	7 years			
Typical class sizes – young children – older children	up to 50 students up to 50 students	around 20 around 25			
Methodology	whole class teaching, teacher centred	child-centred, individualised approach – especially for young children			
Type of learning valued – co-operative – independent – analytical – rote – critical thinking	competitive, strong in maths and science, examination driven	collaborative, child-centred, problem-solving			
Relationship between student and teacher – respectful – informal – distant	distant, respectful	informal, friendly, co-operative			
Involvement of parents	strong support of mother outside school	inclusive partnership view of schooling			
Disciplinary methods – corporal punishment – rule-based – mutual respect system	strict, rule-based, corporal punishment on occasion	mutual respect system			

Mobility and change

When you are new yourself it is sometimes difficult to realise that up to one third of the class you teach may also be new at the beginning of the school year. This is because students in international schools tend to move on with their parents very frequently and may also leave and enter school throughout the year. For instance, the average student stay in many schools is between two-and-a-half and three years.

In view of this constant mobility, it is good practice to start the year by setting out to parents as well as students your and the school's expectations very clearly. You should also not forget that the same process is necessary for new students as they come into the class during the year. It is one of the challenges of working in an international school that the class at the end of the year is invariably not the same as the one you started with at the beginning of the school year.

It is helpful to take all students on a tour of the school and to explain the typical routines of the school day. Probably you will want to assign students who already know the school well to act as partners or 'buddies'. Another vital procedure is to explain how things work in areas such as discipline, homework, diary keeping, marking or grading, assessment, absences, acquiring PE kit and so on. This is important in view of the differing expectations and experiences of both parents and students. Time spent at this point in establishing shared understanding about basic procedures will avoid many problems later on.

Especially with second language students, but also with any new students, you should not assume that one explanation will be sufficient. It is helpful to employ the same phrases and vocabulary using the school's terminology when students are expected to carry out a new procedure, and to be very consistent in your classroom practice for the first few weeks.

The layout of the classroom – what does it say about how we teach?

The placing of desks and tables in a classroom may seem a matter of course for those of us with experience of teaching in English-speaking countries. In most international school classes, some students might have different views on the norm for the layout of a classroom as you will see illustrated in the diagrams below. More significantly, the layout of the classroom reflects the type of teaching and learning that is carried on in that classroom.

Typical primary classroom layout in an international school

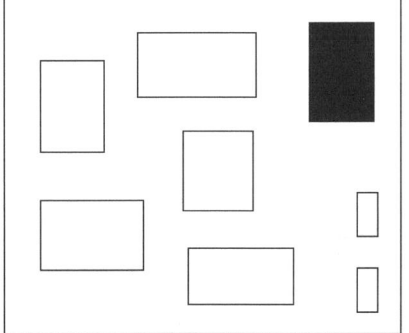

'Traditional' classroom layout

The consequence for teachers in international schools is that we have to let students know exactly how we expect them to behave in our classrooms and we have to teach them how to meet those expectations. For example, this type of modelling/teaching is especially necessary in class discussions and in collaborative learning groups. It is unlikely that students who have been taught while sitting in rows of desks facing a teacher have had the experience of a participative approach.

The number of readily accessible books and computers is also an issue. Some students are not used to the degree of provision and access common in many western-style schools. They must be taught explicitly how these features can be integrated successfully into their studies and given many opportunities for supported practice.

The bottom line is that, at the beginning of the school year, you cannot make any assumptions about the learning modes of your students. As the year develops you will gain a clearer understanding of how each student functions, and where it is necessary to offer explicit support. The message for teachers in our classrooms remains: let your students know what your expectations are and give them the means to be successful in meeting those expectations.

Discipline and behaviour

New teachers, new students and new parents arrive in an international school with varying views of what acceptable behaviour is and how discipline should be maintained. These views cover the spectrum, ranging from a structured, rule-based approach, perhaps backed-up by corporal punishment, to an extremely liberal approach that allows students an almost total freedom of expression and choice. Most international schools opt for a middle way. Policies and rules have been designed to create a community where individual students can flourish within an ordered society that reflects the mission of the school. The approach to discipline tends to be based on discussion and the sharing of ideas. In most schools, it is only after these means have been exhausted that more conventional sanctions, such as missing recess and, ultimately, suspension are imposed.

As a new teacher you will need to reach a rapid understanding of what the basic expectations about behaviour and discipline are in your particular school. It is your responsibility to help colleagues enforce the school rules. It is essential to explain very clearly and as often as necessary, how you expect your students to behave and what will happen if they infringe the basic rules.

The problem for many of our students from more 'traditional' school systems is that our expectations may be unfamiliar and unclear. They will find it strange and confusing that for some activities it is necessary to move freely around the room and to talk to classmates. They will be even more unaccustomed to the concept that it is allowed and even desirable on occasion for one student to help her/his neighbour in completing a piece of work. It is not surprising that some students from traditional systems misread our approach to discipline and do not perceive our unspoken rules. Some students are even rather scornful of a system that has few external sanctions.

Teachers need to be sensitive to the range of cultural attitudes that may exist in their classroom. Some students will feel uneasy about the informal relationship between students and teachers. Some young children, used to a different degree of distance between themselves and teacher, will not know how to act if a teacher is overly sympathetic, in the case of a playground accident, for example.

"I assure you, everything is under control..."

The bottom line for teachers in the areas of discipline and behaviour is to avoid mysteries. Clearly spell out your expectations and be ready to intervene at an early stage when a new student seems not to have understood the system.

Communication with parents

Later in this book, we will expand on the topic of international parents. For the moment, we want to underline the importance for classroom teachers of the relationship with the parents. Appearing ready to talk and to communicate about all aspects of school life is an essential aspect of working in international schools.

The beginning of the school year sets the tone for what follows. Indeed, experienced teachers know that the first meeting with parents is very important in establishing a positive relationship for the upcoming year. For new teachers, though, this is just the time when they themselves may be feeling rather uncertain and insecure. The trick is to appear cheerful, kind and competent, even if you don't always feel those things. You may not know the answer to every question immediately, but you need to express a willingness to find out quickly and to get back to parents, without fail, as soon as possible.

As the year progresses, you need to have in place some regular means of communicating with parents (and older students) about the academic programme of your classroom and about forthcoming class events. It is the custom in most international schools to appoint room parents for the younger children's classrooms. They provide support for class trips, arrange social events, and so on. Make this person your ally. Without being indiscreet, engage him or her in your plans for enriching the basic programme of your class for the year. Most parents respond very positively to being allowed to have an active role in their child's schooling.

In general, the social interaction between families and teacher tends to be more extensive and informal than in national schools. You may be asked to students' homes or to formal receptions, and many parent teacher associations arrange a magnificent teacher appreciation lunch each year. In turn, you may be surprised to learn that many international schools provide a list of teachers' home telephone numbers so that parents can contact them at home.

Practical matters: health, absence, dress, food, transport

There are some practical issues that arise in international school classrooms that may be unfamiliar to new teachers. In relation to health, for instance, students who have lately moved to a new country and school may readily succumb to new infections. Many students, second language students in particular, become fatigued from the effort of adapting to their new circumstances. Other students show physical symptoms of stress. Moslem students may fast during Ramadan, when they may be less able to concentrate or perhaps may be short-tempered. It is a good practice to note any entrenched health problem and to communicate it in a non-alarmist way to parents.

You may notice also that families from certain cultures have differing attitudes to health matters. Some families send students to school who are really ill, not wanting them to miss a day's schooling. Other parents keep their children at home for quite slight reasons such as a late night. Some parents are noticeably more relaxed about school attendance for their daughters than for their sons. It is the custom in international schools to be understanding of these views and only to intervene or

The nature of international schools

question the parents' decision when a student's academic or social well-being is obviously suffering.

Other reasons for a student's absence may be unfamiliar to new teachers. Students in international schools frequently arrive a day or two late at the start of school and may leave early. Many students take days off for religious holidays or important home-country examinations. Other students may take time off from school to go on a trip with their parents or to return to their home countries for extended periods of time. In many cases these periods of absence are for family reasons, and in all cases the parents feel the absences are justified.

Schools, in general, accept a certain amount of absence, if missing time at school does not noticeably disadvantage the students. You are expected, as a teacher, to go along with this thinking and within reason to help students make up any work that they have missed.

Other practical areas can cause distress to students and their families because of differences of viewpoint among the various groups in a class. Most, though not all international schools, have a predominant group of students. Differences from this mainstream group, in areas such as food, dress and social life, are a continuing source of potential difficulty. It is up to the teacher to try to avoid awkward situations. Some typical examples are the possibility of a student coming to school dressed differently for a concert or ceremony, or when a parent provides a snack that is unfamiliar to many of the students in a young children's classroom.

This is why communication with all parents is so important. You need to think ahead at all times and to let students and parents know explicitly what is expected of them. Do not be afraid to ask experienced and effective colleagues about any pitfalls that may be associated with an up-coming event.

Another area where new teachers need to be very aware from day one relates to the question of student transport to and from school. New students tend to be very anxious in the first days in a new location, especially in a big city. They probably cannot speak the language and certainly do not know how to use the local transport. Many don't know exactly where they are living. They are absolutely dependent on you to get them safely to the appropriate means of transport. For new teachers, the bottom line is that you do not allow a student to leave your room at the end of the day without being entirely clear about how she or he is to get home.

Assessment at the beginning of the school year

New students in international schools arrive in our classrooms with a variety of educational experiences and histories. It is always very helpful to have read through each student's file before school starts and to refer back to this file when necessary. This first reading answers some of the basic questions: how long has the student been in school? How many times has she/he moved? What is the student's linguistic history? Further information in the file may give some insights into the student's learning profile and level of achievement.

Teachers, however, need to get their own understanding of a student's level of functioning. In areas such as mathematics and English, they need to know how far the student has moved along the learning continuum and where the sequence of their learning has differed from the programme of the new school. In each subject area, they need to gain an understanding of the main topics and themes that the student has studied and what skills she or he has practised.

Any assessment that is carried out, therefore, has to take account of these possible variations in experience, and supply teachers with useful information on which to base their future instruction. Most schools have such an assessment procedure in place. It is possible though, that you may have to carry out your own investigations. If that is the case, the key words for you are variety and breadth. You will need a wide range of different types of assessment in order to illustrate the sequence of a student's learning and her or his present level of achievement.

Several practical points should be noted:

1. From the teacher's point of view this initial baseline assessment is essential if future instruction is to be as effective as possible. Parents, though, are quick to feel that their children are not engaging in new work. It is wise to avoid taking too long over this assessment phase. Try to establish the basics and accept the fact that a full understanding of a new student's learning profile and educational history will necessarily take several weeks.

2. Explain to students and parents that this assessment procedure is primarily aimed at establishing the student's place on the learning continuum. It is not a question of passing or failing.

3. Show extreme discretion in your assessment of second language students. They are always a special case. Consult your ESL teachers about any placement issues.

Second language students – personal and cultural histories

Most classes in international schools contain students for whom English is not their first or home language. Of these students, some will have attended English-medium schools before, while others may be beginner speakers of English. The presence of these students is the norm in international schools and the management of the class must take account of their needs as a base-case.

Within this group of students you may find variations in:

- levels of English competence;
- a single student's proficiency in speaking, listening, reading and writing skills;
- ability and aptitude;
- levels of motivation;
- the students' readiness to take language-learning risks;
- the students' abilities to cope with language-learning challenges;
- the levels of students' competence in their first language;
- the students' abilities to perform higher-level learning tasks in any language.

Teachers have to plan and teach in ways that acknowledge diversity as they must cater for a broad range of aptitude, ability and motivation both within the second language population of a classroom, and among the speakers of English as a first language.

Most schools offer support for ESL students in sheltered classes, in separate 'pull-out' programmes or within the classroom. But it is classroom and subject teachers who are responsible for these students for most of the day and who must adapt their programme and materials so that the needs of all the students are met. In all international schools ALL teachers are teachers of English as a Second Language. The strategies, sometimes known as differentiation, that allow teachers to cater for all their students are more fully referred to later in this book.

Achieving balanced bilingualism

The ideal outcome for students who speak other languages at home and are being educated in English for example is for them to emerge as balanced bilinguals. In other words, the aim is not for English to overwhelm or, in the worst case, to replace a student's mother tongue, but for it to become an additional and valuable tool in her or his language repertoire.

To achieve this goal of balanced bilingualism, teachers need to be positive about parents' and students' efforts to maintain their home language studies. Attendance at extra classes inside or outside school sometimes results in tiredness and the occasional missed homework. It is wise to be understanding about this situation.

Students need to keep up their studies in their home languages, not only in the case of balanced bilingualism, but also because most will return to their home education system where they will continue to learn in their own language. Many students also need to follow their national curriculum since there are key examinations that they are required to take in order to progress through their home systems.

A student's move into an English-medium school may have another undesirable effect. The student may start valuing her or his own culture less than the predominant English-speaking culture of the school. There are two possible causes for this. The first is that the English-speaking administration and teachers in a school often exemplify the values and customs of their English-speaking culture and unconsciously transmit these views in all their activities.

The second possible cause is that students from other cultures feel that they must overtly adopt the modes of the English-speaking school culture in order to be part of the group. In doing so, they may learn to value less their own culture. This is a sad outcome for our students, and the opposite of what is set down in most schools' mission statements. Class teachers can make a significant contribution towards ensuring a more positive outcome by creating an environment where the experiences and lifestyles of all the children are integrated into every aspect of class activity.

Host country students

Most international schools, except those where the local government forbids it, have also some host country students. For classroom teachers, the presence of these students is accompanied with some distinct issues. A significant factor is the proportion of host country students in the classroom.

If there are relatively large numbers of these students, their impact on the life of the classroom will be the greater. The host language will no doubt be widely used, and perhaps for these students a lack of progress in the language of instruction may become an issue. Socially, these students tend to become the mainstream group and other students may remain on the periphery. Classroom teachers in this situation must do their best to set guidelines about the use of language and must try to incorporate fully students from other backgrounds.

Where there are only one or two host country students in a class, the position is reversed. These students may find that they remain outside the mainstream social life of the students who are accustomed to integrating rapidly into a new social scene. They may also become the recipients of all the remarks, positive and negative, about the host country. Teachers need to watch that a balance is kept in this area. It is a positive strategy to encourage host country students to offer insights about their culture and way of life, but we need to guard against allowing one or two students to be placed in the position of constantly defending their culture and country.

Creating an international classroom

Many papers have been written in an effort to describe an international education. No satisfactory definition has yet been reached. The one element that most educators have agreed on is that effective teachers in our schools can be described as being 'internationally-minded'. Being internationally-minded means being constantly aware of the diversity of viewpoints and experience in your classroom and integrating that diversity into all aspects of classroom life.

As a new teacher, even if your school consciously subscribes to one or more national systems, it is possible to incorporate in meaningful ways, references, examples and materials from a broad spectrum of cultural and geographical backgrounds. The Internet is a valuable tool in this respect. It is important to place value on the experiences of all the students and to use that experience to enrich the teaching and social activity in your classroom.

Research has shown, however, that it is teachers and students themselves who most exemplify this quality of being internationally-minded. In other words, it is the people who make a school international. It is your ordinary conversation, the stories you tell, and the references you make to your own experiences of relocation, travel and language learning that convince students they are in the presence of someone who is something more than national. Shared talk about dislocation and the need to adjust to new places, cultures and languages is very valuable in validating the experiences of all the students in a class.

Chapter 3

The nature of international school families

"If everything strange becomes familiar to the expatriate, it is also true that everything familiar becomes strange."

Canadian journalist

Any international move goes together with higher levels of anxiety.

Expatriate families

When a family moves around the world, the one constant in the child's life is the immediate household, parents and siblings. They give comfort and continuity, and set the child's standards of what is normal, good, and likely to endure. Of course the school is an important social centre, but it may take some time to build the links. If you are to be an influential person in the child's life, you too must become a trusted part of the child's world.

Many mobile families come to have an especially intense pattern of relationships, in which the mother is central. Generally it is still the father who is posted to an exciting job abroad, and he will be immediately whisked off on a tour of local operations. This leaves the mother, who is missing friends, family, colleagues and career, to establish a home in a strange society in which she is a fumbling novice. And still everyone leans on her for emotional support! You too are just getting the hang of things, but she will look to you for reassurance. At the outset you may not be able to answer all her questions, but "I will find out and get back to you" is fine. You just need to show professional competence, sensitivity, and willingness to take their viewpoint seriously.

Experienced expatriate families often become experts at mutual support, but there are unseen family members who are also influential. The families may be missing grandparents, parents' siblings, and even pets, which were left with neighbours. They may feel uneasy about elderly or sick relatives who were left at home. Invisible, seldom mentioned but never out of mind, these figures are a source of both strength and vulnerability. Children and parents may have anxieties and guilt about absent relatives which surface suddenly at moments of stress.

Expatriate families may support one another. For example, a new Japanese child may already have been introduced to classmates if their fathers work for the same company, or if they have been enrolled at the local Japanese Saturday school. Through this kind of contact the family culture may be reinforced by the community culture.

Family culture

...personal and cultural histories...

It is within the family that your students first learn what is the right thing to do and say. Your students try to be good children in the eyes of their parents, and so they develop the same set of values. This set of values is the culture of that family, and it is guarded by strong emotions. Your student feels security and happiness when being a 'good child' and feels uneasy when disobeying these deep rules. She or he will have loyalty and affection for the parents and elders who taught them those rules.

If you encourage children to do things which conflict with family traditions they will feel uncomfortable. It seems disloyal to do something grandparents would not approve of – like speaking out in class – even if the teacher asks them to do so. So if children are slow in following your directions you need to remember that their early cultural training is the strongest guiding influence in their lives.

We teachers need to introduce children to the rules of our classroom, which may be unfamiliar to them. We hope the other children who are 'good students' will become good friends of the newcomers. This will help them to join in and all be 'good students' together. But at first it is important to explain that 'this is how we do things here', and show that it makes the class business more efficient or more fair. A child who has made many moves will not be too troubled, and can revert to family values when they go home in the evening. But never forget that 'being good' is an emotional business. You will be reminded of this from time to time in your own life. We, who thought we were so grown-up and competent, can be reduced to frustrated impotence just by not knowing which queue to join at the post office!

Parental expectations

Family culture leads each family to expect something slightly different in life. If the school doesn't turn out as the families expect, they will be disappointed. Especially with first-movers you may find yourself dealing with frustrated and bewildered parents who don't understand what the school is doing, or why it is doing it. This is most obvious if the school calls itself British or American and they are of that nationality. On the other hand, if the school has developed its own 'international' character it is bound to be unfamiliar to everyone in some way that will need explanation.

The first thing is to show you take them seriously. If they are personally hurt or hostile, try to defuse the issue by showing that you and the school are only trying to help the children, and that you may have to respond to a variety of needs. After that it may be school policy to direct them to some senior colleague. Otherwise, it is for you to listen to their worries. This process is, in itself, reassuring and you might try to explain what it is that your school thinks is most practical and useful to do. At all costs avoid an argument which leads to an ultimatum from which there is no graceful exit for either party.

The best course of action is to keep in close contact with parents, so you can explain unfamiliar aspects of the school as they appear. Of course, you will need to understand what is going on yourself. Since the parents' questions are based on their own – often unbelievably different – understanding of what education ought to be, it may be hard to answer without knowing their fundamental expectations. Once again, if you have colleagues from that culture, they can tell you what the issue is and why it matters so much. It may simply be that the family has never experienced a private school before, and that in the family's country the fact their child attends an international school would lead the family to expect a special treatment.

Language

Cultures are passed on through face-to-face social communication, so language is at the core of culture. Wise families value language as it is the key to maintaining the cultural identity in which they feel secure, and vital for satisfactory repatriation. Many international schools support this with mother-tongue classes, which also provide a cultural focus. Even if visiting the international school means the child might think she or he is moving from the less developed world to the more developed world, the family should be advised to keep up the mother tongue as it is the link to so much of their deep identity.

Religious beliefs, just like language, food and clothing, are also at the heart of cultural identity. There is a minefield of mistakes waiting to be made over unclean animals, fasts and festivals, prohibited physical contact, and we all make them from time to time. We may be accustomed to bringing deep feelings into the open and 'dealing with' them, but this is upsetting in many communities. Do, before undertaking adventurous social or psychological things with a class, air your plans to that experienced colleague who is your regular 'second opinion' in order to avoid trespassing on sensitive family territory.

International school parents

Earlier chapters have alluded to the role of parents in the school. It is in everyone's best interest if international school teachers try to understand the situation in which their pupils' parents find themselves.

The nature of international school families

Many parents experience high levels of anxiety about the predicament in which they have placed their children. After all, it is generally a parent's career move that has precipitated the overseas move. This can be a source of guilt for many parents who have uprooted their children from familiar school surroundings and moved them into a strange and possibly foreign environment where they may face tremendous challenges. Parents themselves may experience all the phases of culture shock, and this may or may not coincide with the experiences of their children.

All the experts agree that the consequences of an international move – a change of job, moving house, separation from parents or adult children, major purchases such as a new car – are all sources of high stress. With an international move, they come all at once! Parents need to be highly flexible if they are to manage this transition, and they may be experiencing a heightened level of anxiety. They may be struggling with the need to adapt while their children may respond by denying their own anxieties in order to protect their parents and prevent them from worrying.

It is not an exaggeration to say that, when international school educators first encounter their pupils' parents, the parents may be at their most vulnerable point and teachers must keep this in mind if parents seem unnecessarily aggressive. Don't take it personally – that same parent may eventually turn out to be a life-long friend!

While most parents, irrespective of nationality or culture, worry about their children's wellbeing and education in general, it would seem that moving abroad makes them worry even more. Be prepared! Parents worry excessively about issues such as placement, repetition of curriculum, gaps in learning and language problems. They may desperately want to impose on you and your colleagues the norms of the national or international school they have left behind. These parents must be continuously educated about the ways of your international school. Be patient, keep your cool, and just keep the lines of communication open.

Remember that parents are thinking not just of the placement in your school, but also about how this experience will affect their child's educational placement when they return home. Listen to these parents, understand their concerns, keep explaining how things work, and keep reassuring them. If you become defensive, things will just get worse. If things are getting out of hand, enlist the support of your department head,

The nature of international school families

principal or school counsellor. Sometimes parents can be reassured by other parents. Learn quickly to identify those parents who seem to be happily adjusted and engaged in the local lifestyle – it may be that another mother taking a worried mother out for a cup of coffee will go a long way towards settling the anxieties.

One important piece of advice is that you make a point of reading the files of your new pupils. So often in international schools pupils are not what they seem. Their experiences can be highly diverse, and background information found in the file can be useful. Sometimes parents have gone to great lengths to provide information about their children, and they become (perhaps rightfully) annoyed if teachers appear not to know about their child's unique experience. This can be an Achilles heel for the teacher! Be informed, and you will be prepared.

Though the school administration in the form of the admissions department and the principals will have made some decisions about placement in a year group, they do not always get it right. On the other hand, sometimes it takes a few days or weeks for new pupils to settle, and so a bit of patience may be required as you make judgements about placement or levels.

Many teachers will spend the first few weeks assessing pupils to establish gaps, strengths and weaknesses, levels of language fluency and maths proficiency. Some schools group by age, at least in the primary years, and necessarily offer a differentiated curriculum. Others group by achievement despite the social problems this gives rise to. However, if you suspect a child is wrongly placed in your class or year, do raise it immediately with the appropriate school authority.

As we explained earlier, each school has its own nomenclature for grades or year groups. Some parents find it difficult to accept placement in what, at first glance, appears to them to be a 'lower' or 'higher' grade or year. Some parents seem to think that in the international school it will be possible for their child to acquire total fluency in English while at the same time skipping ahead a year!

Of course pupils moving between the northern and southern hemispheres are often faced with a significant change in the school year, which means repeating or skipping half a year, or skipping ahead. It is for these reasons that most international schools expect teachers to use a degree of differentiation or individualisation in their delivery of the curriculum.

Some dedicated parent seem to be camping in the school...

Depending on their cultural backgrounds, you may have some parents who wish to visit your classroom almost on a daily basis. They want to volunteer at every opportunity, and in fact parent volunteers, properly managed, can be very helpful to an over-worked teacher! By contrast, some parents may come from a culture where they would never dream of going anywhere near the school, where parents have no role to play in the educational process. In such cases you may become frustrated at the lack of response or involvement from the parents. Another dilemma is presented by those affluent families who seem to leave matters of child-rearing and education to their nannies, governesses, private tutors, drivers, maids and secretaries. This is something you should discuss with your principal. To what extent is the school content to have teachers interface with 'employees' of the family? This can be extremely frustrating for a teacher who wants to engage the parents in their children's education.

As a teacher in an international school, you will encounter a wide range of family situations. While it is probably still most common to find a traditional family where the father is the professional 'assignee' on overseas assignment, more and more mothers are the catalyst for the move. Increasingly one also finds situations where both parents have careers – perhaps high pressure jobs involving a lot of travel. But also one encounters single parents, parents with partners (both heterosexual and homosexual) who are not the parents of the child, and even occasionally families where the child is not biologically related to either parent due to multiple divorces.

Sometimes children come from cultures where the parent (usually the father) may have more than one spouse and the child has many 'brothers and sisters' who are in fact half-siblings or even cousins! In a multicultural environment, these can present interesting challenges if 'family' is a topic of study or discussion in the classroom. On the whole, though, there are probably more conventional families in the international expatriate community than in other settings. Never be surprised at what you may learn from your pupils and your families!

International school children

The impact of mobility

....the ups and downs of mobility...

One of the defining characteristics of most international schools is the high mobility of their student populations. The changes these children experience have a profound effect on their lives as they are faced with a new school, new home, new neighbourhood, new culture and often a new language all at once!

Children who move frequently from country to country are often referred to as 'global nomads' or Third Culture Kids (TCKs) and usually develop certain characteristics as a result of growing up in more than one country and culture. Their experiences present to them both tremendous benefits and significant challenges. It is essential that every international school educator should gain an understanding of the issues faced by families on the move and help support them in the school and in the wider community.

At any given time students in your school are going through some stage of the process of transition involved in moving to another country. This means that there are always students who are newly arriving, those who are beginning to settle in, those who feel a sense of belonging in the location, and those who are preparing to leave for their next destination, possibly repatriating to their passport country. It is indeed a challenge to meet these differing needs at the same time!

It is therefore important to learn about the transition stages and the experiences associated with them. David Pollock has developed a model of the transition process, which helps us understand the experiences encountered when moving from one culture to another. It includes the following five stages:

Involvement – In this stage we have a sense of belonging to the community we live in, and we feel settled and comfortable.

Leaving – Once we learn we are moving, we enter the leaving stage. This stage brings many mixed emotions as we say goodbye to people and places that are important to us, and begin to focus on the future.

Transition – This stage begins once we actually leave one place and ends once we arrive at the new destination and make the decision to become a part of it. Life is quite unpredictable during this stage and is characterised by chaos and anxiety!

Entering – During this stage we feel particularly vulnerable as we begin to learn about the new country and culture in which we are now living. Emotions may fluctuate as we begin to adjust to our new lifestyle.

Re-involvement – In this stage we finally have a sense of belonging in the new community.

(See Pollock and Van Reken, References)

Once you become familiar with these stages you will be able to see where your students and their parents are in this process and support them accordingly. Children and their parents may respond differently to these stages and move through them at different rates.

There are many factors that affect a child's response to moving, such as personality, the destination, the amount of prior notice to the move, and the opportunity to say goodbye and bring closure among others. Children's attitudes towards the move also differ depending on their age and the number of times they have moved before. In particular, young children may feel disoriented once their familiar routine is disrupted, and teenagers may be quite angry about moving as it is difficult for them to leave their established social network.

The nature of international school families

Children's attitudes towards the move often reflect the attitudes of their parents. You may find that as they pick up their parents' stress your students behave differently at home than at school. It is important to recognise that some children have the additional burden of interpreting the new language for their parents.

As the child's teacher you will have a key role in helping the entire family adjust to the new school and culture, or prepare for departure.

What can you do?

- Be aware of where you are in the process of transition and consider sharing your own experiences with your students and their families;

- Learn about the experiences of transition and international mobility by reading professional literature and attending seminars on the topic;

- Provide activities for your students that help facilitate their arrival at and departure from your school. On arrival you might assign a buddy, explore the local neighbourhood with the class, or make a welcome poster;

As arrival is a particularly sensitive time, be sure to choose activities that are culturally appropriate for each student. For departing students you might have the class make a memory book, write cards, sign a T-shirt, or present the child with an appropriate gift from the host country. You and your class can create your own rituals!

- Establish a sense of community in your classroom. While this is important in any school, it is of paramount importance in international schools. This helps give children a sense of security at a time that can be particularly stressful;

- Get to know your students. Find out about their backgrounds and life experiences, and who they are as individuals;

- Demonstrate your interest in learning about your students' cultures. Look for opportunities to incorporate their backgrounds, knowledge and experiences into class discussions, projects and assignments in different subject areas;

- Provide opportunities for your students to reminisce about the special people and places they behind. It is important to establish a balance between affirming your students' past experiences and helping them adjust to a new place;

- Help departing students plan ways to say goodbye to teachers and friends, and gain a sense of closure before they move. Encourage them to consider ways to keep in touch with the school and friends they have made;
- Make sure you address the feelings and needs of the children who remain behind once a friend has moved away. These children experience significant transition adjustments as well;
- Include transition education in your curriculum. Provide opportunities for your students to learn about the experience of transition and to develop strategies to manage change successfully.

As children and their families adjust to living in another culture they are likely to experience some degree of culture shock. This may be particularly difficult for some children and it is important to be aware of signs of stress. In more extreme cases, these may include anxiety, irritability, aggression, withdrawal, physical ailments, confusion or depression. While experiencing culture shock is normal you may need to engage the help of your principal, the school counsellor or an outside professional if the symptoms persist for a prolonged period of time.

Practical issues of mobility

Given that international schools serve the needs of the expatriate community, children in international schools may move at any point during the year. While there is usually advance notice before a new student arrives at your classroom door, sometimes a move can happen very quickly and you may be surprised suddenly to find a new face in your midst. Be prepared to welcome students throughout the year and help them engage in the life of the classroom and the life of the school.

It is important to note that children can leave the school community just as quickly, sometimes without the opportunity to say goodbye. This is very difficult for both the child who is leaving and the children who are left behind. Look for ways to help all of the children say goodbye effectively. Your pupils could write goodbye notes to the student after he or she has left, or send on a class project that you may have been working on, or a yearbook.

There can be great differences between international schools and the national schools your students have previously attended. In fact there are often great differences between international schools themselves!

Children in your classes will probably arrive having widely different school experiences and educational backgrounds. It is therefore essential to assess your students carefully upon arrival and throughout the year to make sure that any educational gaps are addressed.

Second language students

Second language children face the challenge of learning English while at the same time adapting to a new culture. There is much you can do to ease the process of adjustment. Take time to learn about the cultural backgrounds of the students in your classes. Learn how to pronounce your students' names correctly (this is so very important!) and how to speak a few words in their language. Establish clear routines in your classroom and incorporate teaching strategies to help facilitate second language learning for your students. Remember that in addition to modifying class work, you may need to give some thought to appropriate homework assignments. (See Sears, References)

The importance of maintaining the home language and culture has long been documented by research. Some students are so eager to fit in with their peers, however, that they resist continuing to learn their mother tongue language. You can play a positive role in helping your students to see the value of maintaining their own language as well as acquiring the new one.

Personal and cultural identity

Children are influenced by the cultures in which they live in significant ways. Some children who grow up living outside their passport country may have a different cultural identity from their parents. They may identify strongly with a particular country they have lived in and of which they have special memories. Or they may see themselves as internationalists, with a sense of belonging to many countries and cultures.

Many children adapt to the international school culture while at school and switch back to their family culture at home. Sometimes the exposure to different values and behaviours at school, however, causes conflict between parents and their children. This is particularly true for older children for whom clothing styles and social activities may clash with family values. You may find yourself in the position of mediating between students and their parents when cultural differences arise.

Social life

...a middle school dance at the beginning of the school year...

International schools are often the focal point of students' social lives as well. Making new friends and fitting in to the new school is of the utmost importance to all children entering an international school. Some children will form new friendships easily while others may have difficulties. While you cannot force friendships, you can help facilitate relationships between your students by assigning buddies or pairing students for project work.

Help your students engage in the life of the school. Encourage them to participate in extra-curricular activities that interest them such as art, music, sport or student council, and to explore the opportunities to join after school activities. Help them to identify community-based activities as well. This is an excellent way for children to engage with the host culture and perhaps form some friendships that will be less transient. You will probably find yourself liaising with parents to facilitate arrangements for after-school activities and your students' social lives.

In conclusion, by providing support and understanding, you can help maximise the benefits and ease the challenges of an international move for the children and families you work with.

Host country families

Many international schools have a proportion of host country families in their community. The only real exceptions to this are those countries where, by law and often for political or perhaps nationalistic reasons, local children are banned from attending international schools. The host country nationals may represent a small proportion of the school community, usually the economic elite of the local country who believe that such an education will lead to higher education possibilities in North America or Europe. Or, they may represent those associated with a certain industry whose employees have the right to send their children to international schools. At the other end of the spectrum, the host country nationals may represent the vast majority of the total school population, to the extent that one may wonder just what makes such a school international.

The way that the host country nationals interact with the rest of the community is almost always a consequence of their collective size within the school population. They may feel isolated and different, living on the local economy rather than enjoying the many benefits shared by their expatriate classmates. Alternatively, they may represent the economic elite of a country and in fact may seem to be more privileged than the expatriate families in the school. Or they may dominate the community to the extent that the school has to adjust its practices to suit their interests, and the expatriates are made to feel like outsiders.

Whatever the circumstances at your school, 'divisions' between the locals and the internationals are rarely in the school's best interest and strategies are needed to minimalise them. The greater the integration, the more rewarding the experience is for everyone concerned. Talk to your colleagues about this matter.

Chapter 4

Programme and curriculum

"The days went on – I could speak a tiny bit of English. I got to know how things work here but it took me loads and loads of time, and I thought that it was harder than getting to know the grammar of English."

13-year-old Japanese girl

Introduction

Teaching in an international school presents a rich opportunity for your personal and professional growth, and while it can, at times, be quite challenging, it can also be creative and inspiring. There will be opportunities to learn from your colleagues and to share with them as well. In this way everyone can add to his or her repertoire of teaching strategies.

The programme and curriculum vary from school to school. In some schools the curriculum is set while in others it is influenced by the mobility of the teachers. Topics and programmes may be implemented only to fall away once the responsible teacher moves on. You will also find a wide spectrum of educational methodologies ranging from progressive to more teacher-directed approaches. While you will be able to express your own teaching style, you may have to adapt to the expectations of the school as well. Flexibility is the key.

It is important to provide opportunities for your students to learn about the culture of the host country including its language, history, geography, art and music. Plan visits to local places of cultural interest such as museums, monuments and theatres.

Pedagogy

IB or American schools tend to be student-centred and encourage students to take an active role in their own learning. They encourage inquiry, critical thinking and problem solving. Other schools may be more teacher-directed.

Programme and curriculum

Teaching methods do not just have to match the customs of the school. We need to be aware of the varied ways that students (and parents) perceive our teaching. It may be hard to accept that most students are trying to be 'good students' in their own way. You can see that people with different ideas about who is responsible for learning will work in different ways, and have different teacher-student relationships. Nordic countries incline towards the democratic 'American' model, central and south European nations to the meritocratic 'British' style.

The 'collectivist' societies of the Far East reach high standards by very hard work, often in teams and have little experience of individual, creative or loosely-structured working methods. For these students, answering questions in class or performing in public are deeply embarrassing, and will be bad habits to take home. Traditionalist societies see learning as a mechanical skill, and find understanding or independent research hard to take seriously, when the 'right' answer is surely in a book somewhere.

'School work': again there is a spectrum of definitions:

• homework is	to practice skills learned in class	to add to accumulated knowledge
• writing is	done in pencil so it may be changed	done in pen, so it must be perfect
• participation is	by contributing to discussion	by listening intently and obeying
• work is	thinking and doing	memorising and writing
• success is	known and celebrated	known but not publicised
• working together is	encouraged by the teacher	seen as cheating
• research is	an initiative exercise	finding the right facts
• assessment is	seeing how they are doing	judging their worth

From west to east there is also a range of valuations of skills relative to facts. In the distance between teacher and pupil, international schools generally are on the liberal extreme of the world's educational spectrum;

many students will be from more traditional systems than the teachers. Some schools try to assimilate all students into their way of learning; others allow some latitude for treating students more individually. How far you can differentiate your teaching within the class, yet be seen to treat everyone fairly, is for you to explore.

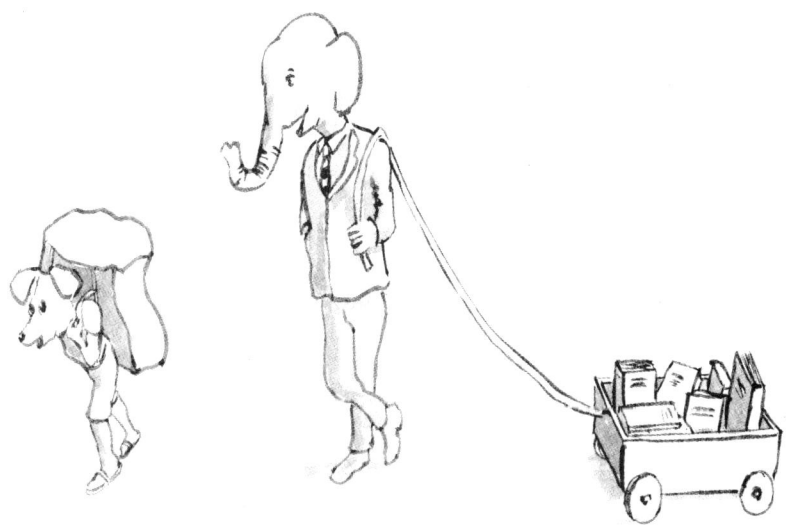

Homework – often a heavy load...

Materials

The type and availability of materials and resources can vary from school to school. While this can make life very interesting, it can also be challenging as it tests your limits of flexibility and creativity! Be resourceful in locating materials and consider using materials published in other countries that may be new to you.

In some cases you may have to develop teaching materials on your own. It is important to be able to rely on your knowledge of your subject, the scope and sequence of its learning objectives, and your repertoire of teaching strategies to develop your curriculum.

Technology resources will also vary from school to school. For example, some schools are equipped to do in-house publishing while others have minimal computer resources, and you may or may not have access to a computer lab.

Assessment

You will find a wide range of assessment methods used in Primary, Middle and High School (Secondary) programmes. These include:

- Portfolio assessment;
- Projects;
- Tests or exams;
- Homework;
- Discussions;
- Oral presentations;
- Written pieces, essays and reports;
- Research;
- Science lab reports;
- Journals;
- Notebooks;
- Standardised tests such as ERBs, IOWA Test of Basic Skills, Key Stage tests.

The grading system also varies from school to school. Some schools use letter grades while others assign numbers. Some schools also use descriptors such as 'outstanding', 'good', 'satisfactory' and 'poor', and give separate grades for effort and achievement. Many schools include the students in the assessment process by having them reflect on their learning and complete a self-assessment. Students may also meet with teachers to develop rubrics or plan learning goals. In some schools, students participate in student-led conferences where they share chosen work and self-evaluations with their teachers and parents. If this is the practice at your school, be aware that some students and their parents may find it unfamiliar and uncomfortable.

Grading and assessment are key issues in international schools. It is important to be able to explain clearly to both parents and students how grades or marks are assigned, and that they know the criteria used. It can be devastating for students who are used to receiving As and Bs to find that suddenly they are receiving lower grades.

It is important to familiarise yourself with the programme offered at your particular school. Read the printed literature the school provides and talk with colleagues to learn about the philosophy, pedagogy, content and materials, and methods of assessment, which comprise the programme.

Primary School

Primary school programmes in international schools usually follow a British, American, national or IBPYP curriculum, or a variation of one of these. Schools that describe their curriculum as 'international' presumably aim to broaden the child's perspective of the world and increase cross-cultural understanding.

The primary school programme in most international schools includes an Early Childhood or Infants programme for children aged between three and seven, sometimes called Nursery, pre K and K or Reception, and graded classes for children up to age ten or eleven. These programmes are usually rich environments in which children learn through play and by interacting with others and with a wide range of educational materials.

Many international schools have a child-centred, inquiry-based approach to education that builds on children's natural curiosity about the world around them. The focus is on learning in meaningful and authentic ways, and in realistic contexts. Children read and write across the curriculum for real purposes and solve mathematical problems they encounter in daily life. They learn about social studies and science to understand more about how the world works. Students take an active role in their learning and opportunities for student choice in deciding what they want to learn are provided. Children are encouraged to discover ways they can contribute to our world and be active, globally-minded citizens.

Many British international schools follow the English National Curriculum, which is separated into Key Stages I (ages 5-7) and II (ages 7-11). The students learn about different topics through a range of activities that are often integrated across the curriculum, although they tend to be more teacher-directed. They also participate in programmes known as Numeracy and Literacy Hours.

Wherever possible, technology is integrated into the curriculum as children design projects and use the computer. Children usually learn to use the Internet as part of their inquiry into the topics they are exploring.

Make sure that the materials you select and display in your classroom reflect the cultures of the children you teach and those in the school. Include a wide variety of books, both fiction and non-fiction, from other countries in your classroom library. Be sure to include materials and projects in your curriculum that enable your students to learn about the host culture as well.

You may find that your core teaching time will vary from school to school as many primary programmes offer foreign language lessons in addition to other specialist classes such as art, music, and physical education. In some schools, students are taken out for classes taught by specialist teachers, and in others the specialist may teach in your classroom. And in yet other schools you may also be required to teach art, music or PE. While all of these classes have an important place in the curriculum, it is an ongoing challenge in most primary schools to find time to deliver the core educational programme.

Middle and High School (Secondary)

As with Primary School, the programmes for Middle School and High School vary from school to school. In some international schools the Middle School comprises grades 5-8, and in others grades 6-8. In some schools the middle school years, ages 11-14, are part of the secondary programme and are referred to as Years 7-9. Some international schools have a discrete middle school programme with a separate middle school faculty, while others share faculty with other divisions in the school. Some High Schools offer the equivalent of a US HS diploma, while others offer the IB. British secondary schools offer the GCSE or IGCSE, and A Levels or AICE (Advanced International Certificate of Education). Some schools offer the national diploma or school-leaving qualification of the host country.

Your head of department may have sent details of your teaching responsibilities to you, but the educational philosophy may be harder to put into words. Many schools are based on US, English or IB programmes. Even if they say they have an "International Curriculum", look closely: are the classes called 'grades' or 'forms' or 'years'? Clues like these show which system the school is most like. And within the formal programme (or program) a thousand details are left to 'common sense', which could mean the values that are common to US or English or local teachers.

Let's assume the school has sent you its programme of study and the syllabus for your classes. If it is a new system for you, you need to start by knowing what the aims are.

Very broadly, US schools aim to deliver an education in which all students can succeed:

- They teach one-year courses, which give a credit towards graduation and college entry;
- Grades awarded by the teacher on all work in grades 9-12 go towards the final GPA (Grade Point Average);

Programme and curriculum

- The Scholastic Aptitude Test (SAT) in Math and English in grades 11 or 12 is the major external exam;
- Grades are all-important; they are calculated, legislated, debated, and gradually inflated;
- There is a strong sense of the students' rights;
- Success is expected, and constantly affirmed and celebrated;
- The few who fail may repeat the course or the year, so the teacher is under direct pressure to give passes;
- Teachers are specialised for certain levels, often following a course book closely;
- Career choice is not necessary until the choice of major subjects midway through college.

By contrast, British schools accept that some students will fail to reach the highest levels:

- Exams set targets that some will not reach;
- Those who fail will drop subjects or choose more modest targets;
- Responsibility for success lies with the nature and nurture of the student;
- The emphasis is on the duties of the student rather than rights;
- Two-year courses lead to external exams or standardised tests in years 6, 9, 11, 12 and 13, rewarded by passes in individual subjects rather than a group diploma;
- Teachers are specialised for a certain subject, often using a textbook for reference;
- Specialised choice of subjects starts in the upper school, well before university entry.

The IB programmes, now covering the entire school career, are used in a wide range of international schools. The original two-year diploma is a demanding pre-university qualification recognised in most countries alongside national certificates. In the last ten years the IB has adopted the Middle Years Programme (MYP) and the Primary Years Programme (PYP), which were developed in international schools with a similar philosophy. You will find them exciting and original ways of teaching, which need continuous planning and training for the entire staff through the year. Your school can give you the outline, but again the way they run the course depends on their kind of 'common sense'.

Your colleagues will probably have different teaching styles from yours, especially if they trained in other countries. They are worthy of respect, and offer you a glimpse of other ways of looking at education.

This table shows some milestones of these three major programmes:

Important tests and *end-of-course external examinations*: (ask colleagues for details)

Age:	USA		UK	IB
17-18 yrs	12th SAT, *AP*		13 *A-level/AICE*	*Diploma*
16-17	11th SAT	HS	12 *AS level*	
15-16	10th PSAT		11 *GCSE/IGCSE*, KS4 SATs	
14-15	9th		10	
13-14	8th		9 Key Stage 3 SATs	IBMYP
12-13	7th SSAT	MS	8	
11-12	6th		7	

If your school implements the IB and the IBMYP, plan to talk with the IB or IBMYP Co-ordinator. They will be able to offer support and tell you more about these programmes.

Pastoral care

Middle and high school years are particularly challenging for children without the added stresses of an international move. During these years friendships with peers mean everything, and fitting in and being accepted by others is of paramount importance. The high degree of student mobility exacerbates the issues facing young people. In addition to teaching your subject it is important to be available to support your students outside the classroom as well.

Enquire about your specific responsibilities for pastoral care. These may include being an advisor, or teaching

...the counsellor's T-shirt?

Health or Personal and Social Education. Sex, and drug and alcohol education, sometimes referred to as 'sex, drugs and rock 'n' roll' are usually taught, and many of the issues that arise can be quite challenging in that they require a degree of cultural sensitivity. Student handbooks will help you to know the procedures and expectations for students.

Schools with bilingual programmes

Some of the most interesting and challenging places to work are schools that offer variations on a bilingual or trilingual programme. Several issues are significant in schools of this kind. You will probably be required to teach only one of the languages, but in any case it will be helpful if you learn something about the key features of bilingualism and second language acquisition. This understanding will inform the teaching of your own language, and enable you to communicate better with your colleagues from the other language sections. Such information is obtainable from the libraries in bilingual schools or via publishers' lists on the Internet.

Further elements that may be strange to a new teacher are the differences in teaching practice and attitudes between teachers in the different language sections. In these circumstances, both sides have to work to achieve effective and mutually comprehensible communication.

Finally, teachers of English in particular may need to recognise that they are being employed to teach the English language rather than to be exemplars of any one English-speaking culture. In a bilingual school, each language and culture carries equal weight and teachers need to be sensitive about any unwitting assumptions they might make relating to the superiority of their own culture and educational practice.

Need for differentiated instruction

Differentiated instruction is an essential practice for international school classrooms where students have a wide range of abilities and experiences. It will allow you to provide for your students' individual learning needs while involving them in work that is interesting, engaging and linked to the curriculum.

Teachers vary learning materials and activities to provide appropriate learning opportunities for all students. The differentiated classroom is student-centred, and students learn to take responsibility for their own learning. Individual learning styles and ongoing assessment help teachers and students make informed choices when they select learning opportunities.

There are numerous strategies you can use to differentiate instruction, and as you become more familiar with them, they will be a highly valuable addition to your repertoire. We recommend reading on this topic, learning from more experienced colleagues and attending professional development workshops on differentiated instruction.

Each of the players needs differentiated instruction...

Special Educational Needs

Children in international schools arrive with a wide range of educational histories and experiences, and it is therefore important that educators are informed about Special Educational Needs.

Special Educational Needs usually refer to a host of learning difficulties that interfere with learning processes and the acquisition of academic skills. They affect reading, writing, speaking, listening, reasoning, mathematical abilities and social skills. A child is thought to have learning difficulties if he or she is not learning at the same rate as the majority of his or her peers.

As it is only a matter of time before you encounter students with special needs in your classroom, it is important to understand the terminology used.

> Some of the terms used to describe learning difficulties are:
> - learning disabilities;
> - specific learning difficulties;
> - dyslexia (difficulty with reading and language;
> - ADD/ADHD (Attention Deficit Disorder/Attention Deficit Hyperactivity Disorder);
> - dysgraphia (difficulty with writing);
> - dyspraxia (difficulty with fine and gross motor skills);
> - dyscalculia (difficulty with mathematics).

Whatever the term used, it is important to understand the nature of a student's learning difficulties and take steps to address his or her particular needs.

The most common learning difficulties are learning disabilities, dyslexia and ADD/ADHD.

Learning disabilities refer to disorders in the central nervous system that interfere with the way information is processed, stored and expressed. They can include difficulty with visual and/or auditory perception, memory, integration and motor skills. They can affect speaking, listening, reading, writing, mathematics and social skills. While they may exist as well, learning disabilities are not the result of a physical disability, impairment, emotional disturbance or environmental factors. Most children with learning disabilities have average or above average intelligence; however, there is a significant discrepancy between the child's level of achievement and overall intellectual ability.

Dyslexia is a learning disability characterised by problems in expressive or receptive oral or written language. Problems may emerge in reading, spelling, writing, speaking, listening, or mathematics. Dyslexia results from differences in the structure and function of the brain. Although visual and auditory processing problems may exist, language processing difficulties distinguish dyslexics as a group. This means that the person with dyslexia has problems translating language to thought (as in listening or reading) or thought to language (as in writing or speaking). (The Orton Dyslexia Society)

ADD/ADHD is a neurobiological disability that is frequently characterised by inattention, impulsiveness, overactivity, disorganisation and social skills deficits.

These disabilities may or may not overlap. If they are left unaddressed, however, they can significantly affect a child's ability to learn and have a detrimental effect on his or her self-confidence and self-esteem.

What signs are cause for concern?

In young children:

- Little vocalisation, cooing or babbling in early months;
- Delay meeting motor milestones, for example, sitting at six to eight months, walking at 12-16 months;
- No real words by age two;
- Not combining words by age three;
- No sentences by age four;
- Echolalic;
- Not responding visually to objects or people in their environment;
- Difficulty retrieving specific words, for example, 'knife' for 'fork', 'stuff' or 'thing' for names of objects;
- Difficulty remembering labels for known objects *eg* colours; 'butter' for yellow, 'grass' for green;
- Difficulty with speech; 'wabbit' for 'rabbit', 'duckth' for 'ducks'.

Difficulty with:

- Reading: decoding, phonics, comprehension, sight words;
- Writing: expressing ideas, syntax, organisation, spelling, handwriting (form, spacing), reversals;
- Speaking: expressing ideas, vocabulary, concepts (directional words such as under-over, up-down, *eg* 'tangerine' for 'tambourine', 'things you put in here to make it work' for 'batteries';
- Listening: processing what is heard, sequence, speaking in full sentences, literal meaning, inability to discriminate from background noise;
- Mathematics: numbers, concepts (*eg* place value, word problems with many steps, sequencing of steps, language of mathematics, visual-spatial difficulties lining up numbers);

- Social skills: body language, social cues, tone of voice, appropriate behaviour, facial expression.

Signs of ADHD:

- Inattention: easily distracted, difficulty concentrating, difficulty listening to and following directions, shifts from one task to another, short attention span;
- Impulsiveness: calls out, rushes into tasks without thinking, difficulty waiting in queues or for turns;
- Overactivity: fidgets, restless;
- Disorganisation: loses things, forgets homework;
- Social skills: lacks awareness and sensitivity to those around them, demands attention, misreads social cues.

International schools vary greatly in terms of the support services they offer for students with special needs. Some schools have learning resource staff who usually combine working alongside children in the classroom and pulling them out for specific lessons, while some schools provide no support at all. Discuss with your principal the kinds of services available at your school and enquire about the availability of educational psychologists in the community. Find out how students are referred for special needs support at your school. It is also important to find out what the school's position is on the use of prescription drugs for ADHD, such as Ritalin, and who is responsible for administering them.

It is important to recognise that some of the characteristics of learning difficulties relating to language can be confused with second language learning patterns. It is usually in noticing that a second language learner is lagging behind his or her second language peers that the question of possible special needs may arise.

The high mobility of international school students and frequent changes of school can make it particularly difficult for special needs to be identified. If you see consistent signs that suggest a learning difficulty, take steps to refer the student for an evaluation. Children can sometimes lose years of support if their special educational needs are left undiagnosed. Engage the support of learning resource specialists as they can help you develop classroom strategies to address your students' special needs. Differentiated instruction will also help you to provide appropriate strategies and activities for all of your students.

For personal or cultural reasons, some parents may be resistant to accepting that their child may have special needs. In fact sometimes parents hope to give their child a fresh start in a new school by omitting the results of previous educational testing identifying special needs from school records. It may be a challenge for you to communicate the importance of addressing these needs. Be patient and respectful, keeping the focus on what is best for the child.

Remember that children with learning difficulties can and do learn, and can be and are successful. The key to a child's success lies with the partnership between parents, educators and specialists working with the child.

Beyond the classroom

Most international schools take advantage of the unique locations in which they find themselves, and teachers are encouraged to plan field trips to local places of interest. In many middle and high schools, students take part in extended trips for team building and/or field studies. There may be opportunities for interesting partnerships or collaborations with local schools, cultural organisations or businesses. Many schools offer ski trips during school breaks and teachers are invited to chaperone these events.

Professional development opportunities

One of the advantages of working in an international school is the opportunity for professional development. There are conferences throughout the year on a wide range of topics and several general conferences are planned yearly. For example, ECIS hosts an annual conference for all educators in November addressing all levels and subjects, and others addressing particular areas of education, such as Early Childhood, IT, ESL *etc.*

We encourage you to take advantage of these opportunities. Not only will you add to your professional knowledge, but you will meet other colleagues from around the world and develop your own professional network. In addition, many of these conferences are held in very interesting places! How about learning about the IBPYP in Nairobi?

Teachers are invited to submit proposals to present at these conferences, and you may wish to consider sharing your expertise at some point during your international school experience.

Most international schools subscribe to a wide range of professional journals. Keep abreast of the current thinking and debate on issues relating to international education.

Postscript: humour/humor

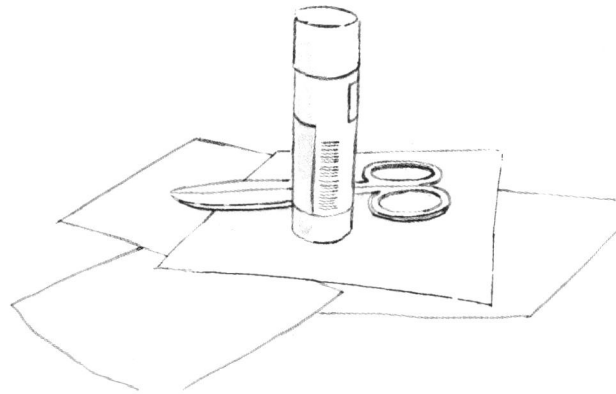

At the end of our sessions in planning, drafting and editing this book we have come to the conclusion that humour is the perfect example to illustrate the levels of comfort or discomfort that can arise from cultural difference.

In our writing group the great disputes centred on whether certain turns of phrase were appropriate. What one or two of us thought were witty and illuminating ways of describing a situation, the others would think were disrespectful and highly inappropriate. What seemed to some to be lightly-veiled comic irony seemed rather insulting to the rest.

These differences about what is humorous are all around us. How many times have we come across a television channel in another language where the audience is roaring with laughter at something that seems banal, unkind, cruel, pointless or just plain unfunny? How many times have we sat in the dentist's waiting room and mulled over the cartoons in *Paris Match*, or some other magazine, trying to understand where the humour lies?

Experienced administrators in international schools often say that they avoid humour in anything they write or speak. The possibilities for misunderstandings are too great. So, does that mean that we are condemned, in international schools, to living in an environment where the talk is bland and lacking in colour and where we dare not open our mouths for fear of offending someone? By no means. The point about adjustment in the face of a new cultural ethos is that you gradually adapt and become accustomed to the new ways that prevail in that group. So, in the case of humour, you begin to tune in and to anticipate what your new colleagues will find humourous. You may even come to find the same things funny yourself.

Humour in international schools does exist and prosper in any case. Our schools tend to be close-knit communities that create their own myths and references and acquire their own brand of humour relating to shared experiences. It is a measure of how successfully you have adjusted to your new surroundings when you can join with understanding in the laughter of your colleagues.

References

Hayden and Thompson (1998), *International Education: Principles and Practice*, Kogan Page, UK.

Pollock & Van Reken (1999), *The Third Culture Kid Experience: Growing Up Among Worlds,* Intercultural Press Inc., Yarmouth, Maine, USA.

Rader and Sittig (to be published December 2002/January 2003), *Children on the Move: Easing the Issues of Student Mobility*, Teachers College Press, NY.

Sears, C (1998), *Second Language Learners in Mainstream Classrooms*, Multilingual Matters, UK.